T0146942

"A great story about how challenges can be laden with gifts when you work on yourself, as well as about taking ownership so that you are making better choices to support yourself and others."

-Clare Corsick

"Jeanne opens up about how her past, curiosity and gumption propelled her to make bold decisions to further her career. She shares how taking risks and finding courage created exciting opportunities that brought out her unique talents and skills that even surprised her. Jeanne's story is inspiring. It will make you laugh, cry, and reflect on your own past experiences. This book is a must read for any administrative professional, especially those who are looking for advice about how to advance their career."

-Linda McFarland

The Divine Intertwines

A light-worker's Spiritual Adventure in Silicon Valley

JEANNE CORSICK

BALBOA.
PRESS

A DIVISION OF HAY HOUSE

Balboa Press books may be ordered through booksellers or by contacting:

Balboa Press
A Division of Hay House
1663 Liberty Drive
Bloomington, IN 47403
www.balboapress.com
1 (877) 407-4847

Because of the dynamic nature of the Internet, any web addresses or links contained in this book may have changed since publication and may no longer be valid. The views expressed in this work are solely those of the author and do not necessarily reflect the views of the publisher, and the publisher hereby disclaims any responsibility for them.

The author of this book does not dispense medical advice or prescribe the use of any technique as a form of treatment for physical, emotional, or medical problems without the advice of a physician, either directly or indirectly. The intent of the author is only to offer information of a general nature to help you in your quest for emotional and spiritual well-being. In the event you use any of the information in this book for yourself, which is your constitutional right, the author and the publisher assume no responsibility for your actions.

Any people depicted in stock imagery provided by Thinkstock are models, and such images are being used for illustrative purposes only. Certain stock imagery © Thinkstock.

Print information available on the last page.

ISBN: 978-1-5043-8693-7 (sc)
ISBN: 978-1-5043-8694-4 (e)

Library of Congress Control Number: 2017913615

Balboa Press rev. date: 09/28/2017

Contents

Acknowledgments

I want to first and foremost thank my soul for showing me the way; bringing me the right people; and reminding me of what I came here for.

My life coach. There used to be a lot of stigma to having a life coach, but we hit the ground running and never looked back. You empowered me, coached me, and helped me build a new foundation from within. I love how we've transformed our sessions into the partnership we have today.

My family. For having the courage to incarnate in these times of change; to find our own unique way in life; and to live our dreams.

My friends, old and new. Your time and energy spent with me has equal contribution to my growth as with all others mentioned.

Beginnings

The inspiration for writing this book came about in quite an interesting fashion. In 2015, I had been asked to speak at an industry event hosted by the Executive Assistant Organization (EAO) on a weekend retreat workshop in Monterey, California.

My prior experience of speaking was limited to anonymous meetings years ago (Alanon meetings), so I was nervous. As I put my slides together, however, things came together quite seamlessly: a first sign, then, that this was meant to be.

As a presenter, I didn't believe in showing slides filled with text, so I found different funny memes to represent the different areas of my career. I wanted to share on the topic of how the divine intertwines at work, and I hoped these stories would resonate with my audience. An audience, mind you, that could be a bit of a challenge to keep engaged and interested, given that they were either personal assistants to high-powered public figures or executive assistants to C-level professionals.

My subject could be touchy, too, as I intertwine spirituality and the divine into my story; faith is very personal matter and likely different for each individual in the room.

After receiving an overwhelmingly positive response to my talk, I checked out of my hotel and began the hour long drive home. I realized on the drive that I had experienced a "meta-morphasis." While reliving the presentation of my career story in my thoughts, I began receiving encouragement to write a book from my spirit guides. Needless to say, it was an unexpected and profound drive home.

So here it is: my career story condensed into a small book. A story I hope resonates with anyone who is at the beginning, middle, or is currently transitioning onto something new. I hope that you receive and feel the validation and inspiration from my story for wherever you are on your path.

Chapter 1

Take That; Rewind It Back

The foundation of my story, as with most others, begins in childhood. What might not run parallel to others, though, is that I was raised with twelve siblings in Santa Clara, California. We were a strong and devout Catholic family growing up in an old, beat-up Victorian house with large bedrooms, a huge yard, and a variety of pets. We played kick-the-can with the neighborhood kids in the summer, and I raised chickens, pigeons, ducks, a goat, and more, with my two brothers.

We were sports oriented, given my father's passion for track and field, and we were a creative bunch that was talented artistically as well as musically, given my parents' love of music and musical instruments.

My father was an architect and talented artist. My mother had a beautiful spirit, but she suffered (triumphantly, at times) with alcoholism; she was a psychic, a birthright activist, a poet, a cancer survivor, and a nature lover.

I strove to be a perfect straight A student and a talented athlete to please both parents and stand out from my other siblings.

On the dark side, we endured late-afternoon to early-morning alcohol-induced rage binges from our mother, who was looking for relief from the stress of raising so many children.

On the upside, we were supported and guided in areas where our parents saw a natural talent to develop.

We also had a stronghold with tradition that was instilled by both religion and our cultural background (French, Italian, and Irish). For years, we sang together on Christmas Eve at our parents' friends' homes all over the Bay area. It was singing where we found heart-centered harmony among us. And it was beautiful.

Our weekends took us on long drives with our parents to explore the California coastline with whale watching, kite flying, sand-duning in Half Moon Bay, and hiking at state parks.

So it is here I began life surrounded by siblings, as I strove to survive competition, envy, frustration, impatience, and insecurity—just to name a few—and doing everything I could to control my environment.

The funny thing is, it was instilled in me to work hard, do for myself, be fair, and go out of my way to help others. I knew at a very young age that I was just surviving, though. Surviving, I told myself, until I was out of the house and could learn how to thrive in life, not just survive it.

As my older siblings moved out and on with their lives, the second half of us were raised (I felt) through the toughest time of my mother's life. It would be her darkest days of alcoholism.

During this time, two of my sisters introduced a few of us to Ala-Teen, another twelve-step program, but I was still in too much of the mind-set of never exposing our secret to others, much less trusting anyone. I was afraid of life. I didn't trust it. I wanted someone to rescue me from the pain and dysfunction of what was at home. I latched onto friends.

My perfection and control issues started very early. At the age of six, I decided I was going to do everything I could to be better than anyone else in school and in sports. This decision came on a day when all of the kindergarten girls had to race each other in separate heats to see who would compete on the last day of school in the fifty-yard dash. I made it through preliminary heats and came in second in the final showdown. I told myself, "Never again. I will always come in first."

It was then that I began competing with voracity in academia and in sports until I got noticed. Before long, I gained a reputation for being better in both sports and classwork than everyone else around me. It was tough to be around me, as I was attached to my own success, yet I had very weak social skills. I didn't trust girls, because I thought they were mean and two-faced. I felt more comfortable with the boys, so I increased the tomboy energy I had developed.

By the time I was a teenager, I had made another decision: that I would continue to survive my circumstances and move out on my own as soon as I was able. I decided I would find a therapist (today, a life coach) where I could stop, take the time to look, transition my people-pleasing behaviors into assertiveness, and do whatever I needed to get my "self" whole. I wanted to get through the anger issues and understand what my feelings really were, so I could get to know exactly who I was. Yes, it was a ton to bite off and chew, but I was determined.

The reason for my determination?

I innately felt there was a lot that I was supposed to do in this lifetime. Not workwise, not so much people-wise, but spiritually. It was important work I was supposed to be doing. I felt, globally, but when? Where? *What?* I didn't come down remembering my *entire* soul's blueprint, so I'd better get onto clearing the human clutter and then maybe I would get somewhere—somewhere I was supposed to be.

Thus began this focus and investment on self-work in my twenties, which, by-the-way, were wrenching. My friends were off at four-year colleges, but by my sophomore year in junior college, I was burned out. My parents said to either continue with school or go to work. So I opted for work.

At the same time, I never felt so lost inside. I couldn't wait to get through my twenties and into the safety of my thirties. So seeking outside help was a good call during this time.

In addition to working, I began attending Al-Anon meetings. And as I continued to attend, year after year, I felt stronger emotionally and a monumentally amount stronger spiritually. I realized these Al-Anon meetings weren't just about the alcoholic, but their principles applied to everyone and every area of my life. This would assist me tremendously in my career life, along with the life-coaching sessions I was doing in tandem.

Chapter 2

Let's Get Metaphysical

I also need to lay the groundwork about the metaphysical side of my spirituality and how it came about.

As a family, we were raised Catholic, but I couldn't get past the guilt and shaming to understand my own faith. I stopped going to church altogether shortly after Confirmation. A few years later, my sister Cathy was getting into metaphysics and going to see lectures on the subject. I went with her to see one of these folks. The speaker's name was Betty Bethards. Betty was a published author and speaker on many topics in the metaphysical world. She would visit Sunnyvale, California, once a month to speak about energy, translate dreams, and share what was to come in twenty years as global shifts and funky weather changes due to the energy ascension on the planet (i.e., what we are experiencing right now). When she was finished speaking, she would allow people to come and ask her a question or two at a table in the back of the room.

Mind you, I was twenty years old, so my questions were mostly focused on—well, boys. Betty laughed once and told me not to worry, because there would be plenty. Right. Well. Um-hem, when? Yeah, I had to know the what's and the whens in my "I do not deal well with unknown factors" mind-set.

But I was also deeply curious in everything having to do with the spiritually "unseen" world and learning to develop my own abilities. It was here, in metaphysics, that I felt I had found a path to my own spirituality, free from the constraints of human-made constructs in this dimension.

It just so happens that Cathy had received a reading from a lady who was clairvoyant. Now for me, this resonated. For some readers, you may have found this in another form. For me, I was automatically drawn to learning more about her and what a psychic reading entailed. So I set up an appointment to meet with her.

When we finally met, I was amazed at what she could tell me. For instance, she could see the two metaphysical teachers I signed up with to learn about energy and more. And she knew that they were *way* too much in my space, thus crossing my energetic boundaries. Some of you may have experienced this in your own lives, and not necessarily through a reading.

I was sold. I still stayed with those teachers until the end of the series of classes I had signed up for, but I started to learn a lot more about energy and holding my space with this other woman every chance I got.

I was starting to feel my soul information and "knowingness" more. And as time went on, I decided to start my search for a therapist who I could work with to get my emotional, mental, and other bodies into balance. It was a selfish act, the most selfish and joyous act I had ever taken. And it would pay off in spades, especially in my career life.

I went through a couple of therapists, as I realized I could manipulate a session easily and hide. I really needed someone who would see through this and call me on it. And I had the courage to find her. Her name is Marta Dawn Peterson. I was her first client.

What I loved about her was that she was clairvoyant and could see through my valences. She had this tangible way of bringing me around in a session to the truth of what was really there, what was really going on. This went past my ego, my resistance, and my defiance. Gently, calmly, and through my protests and rebellion. She is truly amazing and adept. She is, to this day, an integral part of empowering me and others to be the fully empowered, badass people we desire to be.

On another note, they say old souls never really need to worry about their careers. This allows them to focus on spiritual growth and development. The Achilles' heel tends to be relationships. This is where soul lessons come through. And come through they do in my case.

Fortunately for me though I have had old souls show up in the form of peers, mentors, coworkers, and bosses who were invaluable in guiding me throughout my career.

Chapter 3

The Start of My Career

To start, my first real job came when I responded to an ad from a marketing research company looking for an administrative assistant. I had been on the search a little while and had a few interviews under my belt. But there was something significant that would happen where I first recognized the divine intertwining in my career life.

I showed up for the interview, and there were two other candidates in the lobby. They had been chatting it up and creating attachments with each other. I instinctively knew not to do this and held my space. The owners of the company came out and told us that we would all be interviewing together in the conference room. I was startled by this new development and adjusted as quickly as I could.

Once inside the room, I sat down on the opposite side of the table from the other two candidates and answered the questions as best I could coming from the co-founders. But at one point, I floundered when giving an answer and took the time to compose myself, get back up, and answer it the way I wanted to. I felt myself letting go and relaxing inside. Something just came over me and I let go. I held my own in that room, along with the two other competitors. I was authentic, accepting, and allowing. Not competing. Not matching the other two candidates' energies. And then I realized I was there - for me.

By the time I arrived back home, there was already a message on my answering machine. I was hired. And they especially liked how I handled my snafu when answering and the resiliency I showed in regaining my composure.

When you're allowing, owning what you know, and being authentic and detached from the circumstance, you get what you want and need.

Chapter 4

Chips in Silicon Valley

After a year or two, I was ready for something bigger. Okay, a bigger company. A place I could enhance my skills and cut my teeth, so to speak. I foolishly quit my job at the marketing research firm with no prospects. So I signed myself up with a number of temp agencies, and after a few interviews, I received a call from the smallest agency for an administrative role in a growing semiconductor company in Silicon Valley.

I interviewed with them and was assigned a role supporting the director of northwest sales as an administrative assistant. After a few months, they hired a marketing communications manager and asked if I would support both the sales director and this woman who would head the marcom department as well as investor relations. I was excited and eagerly accepted the promotion. By this time, they had hired me away from the temp agency. At this point I was into my early twenties and had a lot to learn about politics, dating, death, family, and a changing world.

I did a lot of my growing up at this company as I was here for 8 years. My coworkers were my friends and family. My bosses were amazing mentors, which taught me how to build relationships. Now this was also the time I decided to start working on myself with the help of a life coach. I was determined to get in there and see what I was hiding and why I was hiding it. I also didn't want to be my behaviors. I wanted to find me— separate from my patterns of behavior—find peace and happiness within while building a new foundation.

After seven years of growing my skill set as an administrative assistant as well as working hard on undoing behaviors that would not serve me, undoing conditioning from society and family, and undoing negative and critical thinking, I experienced a devastating couple of events.

In December of my sixth year at this company, a coworker was killed in an airplane crash. I had never known death or grief in adulthood. It was a shock to my system and something I could not come to terms with. But the divine was intertwining, especially here. I walked step by step with my life coach to understand and move through the process of dealing with shock, grief, and death. And it would help me for what was to follow.

Chapter 5

The Shock of My Life

The following month, I received a devastating call at work. At this time, I was a senior administrative assistant supporting the vice president of desktop display graphics. The call was from my sister, who asked me to go to a private room to speak to her. I thought I knew what I should be bracing for. In my mind, she was going to tell me that our mother had passed away. She had been failing in health in recent years, so I asked her right off, "Is it Mom?"

"No," she said. "It's Dad."

A thousand thoughts ran through my head. My mom had battled alcoholism, breast cancer, and raising us kids. But my sister was saying that it was ... my dad? *Wha ... Why?* I thought.

"Is he okay?" I asked.

"No. He had a heart attack this morning. He didn't make it. He's gone."

I was in shock. I couldn't catch my breath. She told me to go to HR to be with someone. I don't remember the rest of that call. I headed to the HR office, but my mind was numb. My fingers had curled up, and I couldn't undo them. They were frozen in shock. The woman in HR was very helpful and knew what to do. She had someone take me home and made sure I was not alone.

The next day, I flew up to Eugene, Oregon, where my parents had retired, to meet the rest of the family who were already there. At times, we each had a spell of grief where it really hit home, and we got a little lost in emotion as the shock wore off and the grief began. It was there, too, that I could see my mother making decisions on a soul level that she would go, too. However, I didn't know that this was what I was reading in that moment until she left us, soon after we had the funeral for my father.

After my father's funeral service, my mother's final hours took place four days later. They were spent with Vince, my older brother at her side at the hospital. Her organs were shutting down, and she was drowning in her internal fluids. The doctors kept updating her status to a shorter timeline as to her eventual passing, so Vince tried desperately to get the nurse on duty to allow all thirteen siblings to call in and say their good-byes. But the nurse wouldn't do it. She refused to help.

And then, the divine intertwined and sent my brother an angel. It was an angel in the form of a new nurse who just happened to come on duty early. She agreed to help and supported my brother so our family could speak to our mother before she passed. So all those family members who wanted to speak to our mother could, and this nurse angel patched each call through to my brother to rest the phone by her ear. We received two minutes each with her. And with the last sibling saying good-bye, she took one final breath in and exhaled into a peaceful passing, never to inhale again.

It took a full year and seeing my life coach three times a week to get through the initial grieving process. When you lose a primary parent, it's devastating. To lose two within weeks of each other, just cannot be explained. You must allow yourself to grieve and process, no matter how long it takes. Acknowledgment of your feelings is critical, and allowing them to flow each day, and year, is crucial.

Chapter 6

Software

There came a time when it was time to leave this semiconductor company. There was a huge downturn in the industry, and folks were leaving in droves or being laid off. The divine had kept me in a safe spot up until this point and until I was ready to make my next move.

It came swiftly: I became an office manager and executive assistant in a small consulting firm in the software industry. Here I learned how to negotiate office space and to create, from start to finish, a management conference that attracted software engineering managers to spend the day together viewing presentations and participating in panel discussions about their industry. It was also a place where I had some of the hardest yet most fulfilling parts of my personal growth.

I was now working at a place where I felt everything I was doing both professionally and personally was scrutinized; I was under a microscope. I resisted and was often called on the carpet for mistakes I made. But with the assistance from my life coach, I was able to begin to respond and differentiate when I was reacting to them as if they were family versus work professionals. It was a huge shift for me because once I understood that they were not my family, there was this energetic relief of sorts. I didn't have to bring the family baggage with me to work and then use my energy to respond. You can imagine how much my productivity began to increase. And, as I became more self-aware, I was able to really start building my professional interpersonal life.

So basically, this was the place where I learned how to build integrity. And it was where I ultimately found my value. To this day, when I run into my former boss and his wife, he apologizes for being so tough, but I always respond by thanking him because I know I couldn't have become the badass assistant I became without him. Some people call this a soul agreement that we have with others who challenge us to become better within. I was able to see how important this one was, as well as grateful.

Chapter 7

Biotech

After more than five years with this company, I felt as though I had mastered the skills there and outgrown them. So I began my search for another job. A recruiter brought me to a biotech company.

I was being asked to interview for the role of executive assistant to a new and board-elected president. I was intimidated going into the interview, as I had heard he was from the east coast, was high profile, and had an amazing assistant there. But somehow, I made it through the interview with him with grace and professionalism and was offered the job.

Because of the work I had done with facing my own professional demons while at my previous job, I was now prepared to own my worth and value fully.

And with what transpired over the next year, I was often called on to remind myself of these two things.

I began my job with focus and determination. I knew that if I walked the walk, it would pay off, no matter what anyone thought of me. I didn't undermine others, I didn't throw others under the bus, I didn't engage in gossip, I didn't play politics. I didn't cross the boundaries of the other EAs. I was inclusive without being a people pleaser. I knew whatever information I needed in order to do my job or understand office politics would make its way to me if I was supposed to know. I didn't need to know everything going on. I just needed to show up and do an extremely great job. In the process, I earned people's trust and respect.

I had access to my boss's email inbox and filtered and responded to his emails. I maintained discretion and was able to see by the inbound emails the politics that were being played out.

This all was very important. One day, about six months after I started, he didn't show up for work. It was the Monday after the holiday party we had the Saturday evening before. He hadn't attended. I couldn't figure out why folks were keeping their distance. But when Monday morning came and he wasn't there, I had to actually unlock his office; when I opened the door, everything was gone. That's when it hit me. He was gone from the company. I was a little freaked out. I didn't care if I had a job or not, but there was the survivalist in me that was sure damn scared.

He called me, we chatted, and he explained everything. He said that if I was okay with it, I could stick around, as there were changes coming.

So I said yes.

Through the course of the next six months, I watched as my peers and coworkers were laid off in phases. I also watched a new CEO and CFO come in and determine whether the company should exist further or not.

In the end, I was the last EA left at this company and was asked to support them. I did. Almost every day, until the decision was made as to what 'chapter' we would be filing the company under, I was setting up board calls for the new CEO and CFO in addition to my other responsibilities. The typical strategy to setting up board meetings and board calls in a normal situation is to schedule them a year in advance, once a quarter, while strategizing availability of complex calendars of these board members. You can imagine the stress involved then when you're tasked with creating a call every single day while coordinating with five other outside EAs supporting those board members.

One was so stressful to coordinate that I ended up having to create a poster-size calendar full of a month's worth of availability of everyone in order to demonstrate who was available.

On the afternoon when a particular board call was finally set up, our acting CEO came out from his office and asked me about it. My back was to him as I sat at my desk. I was relieved that it was finally now set up, but I couldn't turn to face him. He asked me another question, and all I could do was sit and breathe; otherwise, I was going to burst out in tears from the combined relief and stress.

He repeated his question, and I just stared at my monitor, trying to keep it together. And when I was finally able to respond, I broke out in heavy sobs. I couldn't turn around. I had made it through so many layoffs that year with finesse, diplomacy, and resilience, and with the support of others who were now gone. But that day, I broke down. I had been doing so well with funneling my grief and other emotions into journaling and life-coaching sessions. But some days, you just can't keep it out of the professional environment.

The CEO was taken aback. He wasn't quite sure how to handle it, but he took me in his office and did a good job of talking me down, without judging and with as much empathy as he could. I came back after lunch and was back on track. Lunch was with a friend, which was very timely. Things always dovetail to the next to get you back on track when you're going with the flow, even with bumps in the road.

In addition, the CFO pulled the CEO aside and reminded him of all that had happened at the company throughout the past year, which helped him better understand what I had gone through.

After a time, they decided to restructure the company. I was told that although the acting CEO and CFO I was working with would not be staying, that I would be asked to stay to support the lawyer who would take the company through the restructuring. The CEO advised me to look for another job. I had been keeping my eye out for available positions anyway and began applying. Within two weeks, and during the end of the dot com crash era, I had a job. Every step of the job search had its own lessons and required a lot of faith, understanding my value, letting go, and utilizing the practice of visualization.

Chapter 8

Got Spam?

So here I was, in a company that survived the dot com crash and was now back in a small hiring phase. I was supporting the CEO, the founder, and the head of operations at a company selling software that kept spam, viruses, and more from getting past your firewall. We were top tier in our space, and it was the beginning of an exciting four years for me. The people who worked here often reminded me of the good folks at the semiconductor company I had worked for years prior. They had a moral compass and worked hard but also believed in work-life balance.

I was the only EA at the time and focused most of my support on the CEO. As we grew, there came a time to hire a CFO. With that, they asked me if I would like to provide coverage to the execs. I suggested having one EA to support both the CEO and the CFO, and I would cover the founder and head of operations. While the new CFO was getting settled, I supported him. We quickly grew and required a few more assistants. In total, we eventually had over 350 employees worldwide and four executive assistants.

In 2006, we announced that we were going to take a year to decide whether to go public or be acquired. During that year, there was a lot of work for our executives to get through. One of the projects that came up was for our business development leader. He was partnering with a very large Internet company, utilizing our spam coverage within their new email application.

The discussion with them turned into an acquisition. Subsequently, in July of 2007, this large internet company announced it would be acquiring us.

Almost immediately, we started working with this company to set up press interviews and send our execs on customer visits to assure them that our product would maintain it's integrity throughout the transition.

In tandem, the acquiring company wanted to give us an initial experience as to some of the benefits of working under their umbrella. One of the first ways of doing this was to facilitate free food, snacks, and other amenities.

I synced with our facilities team and their kitchen facilities team as well to coordinate this effort. It was the first time I was put in the lead of what was in my mind a large-scale operation.

At this point, I should mention that I had been supporting the head of operations, plus the company's founder. It also became very clear that I was going to be extremely busy during the transition process.

This intranet company had launched its calendar and email app, and it was not as robust (at the time) as the suite we were used to. Dealing with this transition was very challenging.

Because I had been so busy on the ground since the announcement, I had to come up to speed quickly, using both our standard suite for email and calendaring, and at the same time work out of this nimble product that this larger company had created. I was also tasked with sharing what I was learning with the other assistants that were still in our office.

Eventually, and as a whole, our new company provided on-site training courses for us. The process of learning a new software tool was key during this time, as it provided me with insights after I had made a paradigm shift.

Once I was established at the new company, I would be called upon to help others make the same switch, including assisting customers who were currently in the trial phase.

When we officially started under the umbrella of

the new company, I was put on a team to help move us to the new company's campus. I worked with a team of close to twenty folks on our side that included facilities, the data-center team people, and telephone techs. We worked together for a few months on how we would transfer our data centers, phones, and all our people down to the main campus.

Once we were all moved in and everything was sorted, they asked me if I would lead the team in consolidating the Enterprise Division into a two-story building. At the time, Enterprise was spread out over a few buildings on campus. I looked forward to taking this on, imbued by the accomplishment of establishing our company onto the campus.

This new move required meeting with each of the department heads to review the proposed plan and to then hand it off for them to plot their teams. The syncs required a special set of people skills, as those I was coming into contact with were from different departments with fundamentally different ways of thinking and with different sets of needs.

Dealing with an engineering leader, for example, is very different from dealing with a sales leader. This process of listening and understanding their needs and priorities also helped me to get to know all the leaders and other people, as well. It was a great exercise in relationship building, and with every level of management and peer. The move was seamless. And the process, learning, and relationship building was setting the stage even further for what was to come.

The next project I took on was working with a team to coordinate the Enterprise Division's sales conference.

My role was as messenger, communicator, and marketer of this event. I also kept track of attendees, providing information to them and letting them know when it was time to sign up and the deadlines they would need to meet for travel and more. It was another opportunity to learn and expand my skill set.

Chapter 9

Enterprising Admins

Every company out there utilizes different software tools for word processing, spreadsheets, calendaring, and email. Enterprise's sales team was selling cloud-based apps, competing against all the large software tool companies.

Selling our apps was an uphill challenge, in that as a cloud-based platform, people not only questioned security in the cloud, but were our apps as robust as their existing environment?

The advantage we had was price point; our suite provided an array of collaborative tools making you more productive, and you didn't need any service agreements, which our competition made their bread and butter on.

Still, our salespeople were up against a lot. And

they had an even bigger challenge when our product was in the trial phase in a prospective customer's environment. The executive assistants there were a part of the trial phase and were oftentimes resisting the switch because they either didn't like change or didn't want to change something that they felt didn't need fixing, and, that they liked to work with.

They just couldn't see the logic nor make the paradigm shift to work with it.

At this point, I had a salesperson come to me and ask if I would talk to one of our large customers in South San Francisco. And, could I bring some of my peers to talk some of their admin assistants off the ledge? Of course I could. We were informed they had been gathering their questions in a spreadsheet.

We picked a date, and I rounded up a couple of other executive assistants, one who supported the founder of another acquired company, and one of the assistants to Enterprise's CEO; a senior executive; and a couple of other highly regarded assistants.

We arrived and were met with a lukewarm greeting. We walked through their questions and explained to them the benefits of going through this change and adjustment. It was absolutely magical to see them actually make the paradigm shift right in front of our eyes, to see why working in the cloud and collaborating in the same space, whether in documents, spreadsheets, or presentations, was so vastly more productive than sending files back and forth to edit.

Because the visit was so successful, they later asked if they could send some more of their admin assistants down to our campus to have a best-practice session there. This appointment ended up dovetailing into events with other customers who were in the trial phase of switching over to our apps and hitting speed bumps as their administrative support pushed back.

The outcome of these initial customer care visits was the creation of best practices to be used while onsite with the customer admin assistants; the creation of a certification program for our own company volunteers; and the creation of an internal web portal where our sales force around the globe could sign up and request onsite assistance for our customers of our now certified volunteers.

Within two years, we had over a hundred certified volunteers worldwide.

It became a very successful program overall and supported a more seamless change with customer admin assistants around the world.

The ability to allow the divine to intertwine in your everyday work life and throughout your career can lead you to far reaching success and an impact you thought you might never imagine.

Chapter 10

Epilogue

You might never know where your co-creation with the divine will lead you. If you look and make changes within, life and the divine will naturally support and respond in ways you may not have expected.

Resources

Author

For contact and speaking opportunities:
Jeanne Corsick
Jeanne.Corsick@gmail.com

Life Coach

Marta Dawn Peterson
Alchemy Academy
www.alchemyacademy.com

Administrative Assistant Organizations

Victoria Rabin, President & Founder
Executive Assistant Organization
http://joineao.com/

Linda McFarland, Founder
Ascend2Success
(408) 206-4564
Linda@ascend2success.com
www.ascend2success.com

Sunny Nunan, Founder
Admin Awards
http://adminawards.com/info@adminawards.com
(972) 498-1755

Printed in the United States
By Bookmasters